THE OFFICIAL GUIDE TO FINAL EXPENSE TELESALES

David Duford

Financial Disclaimer

The information contained in this book is for educational and informational purposes only and should not be considered financial or investment advice. While the strategies and insights provided may be beneficial, results are never guaranteed. Many individuals in the industry may not achieve the desired outcomes, and a significant number of agents may fail despite having access to training, leads, and resources.

Success in this field depends on various factors, including but not limited to individual effort, dedication, market conditions, and the ability to implement the concepts discussed. Readers are encouraged to conduct their own research and consult with financial professionals before making any business or investment decisions. The author and publisher disclaim any liability for any losses or damages arising from the use or reliance on the information provided in this book.

About The Author

David Duford is an author, YouTube influencer, and owns The DIG Agency. Starting as a licensed final expense agent in 2011, David started The DIG Agency in 2013 and gradually began to build his agency larger and larger with each consecutive year.

As of 2024, The DIG Agency has recruited 5,000+ agents, has created dozens of six-figure income earners, and mentors multiple seven-figure insurance agencies. David resides in Chattanooga, Tennessee, with his wife and four kids, and is an avid jiu jitsu student and weightlifter.

Contents

Introduction vi

Chapter 1: My Story 1

Chapter 2: The Basics Of Final Expense Telesales 7

Chapter 3: Short- and Long-Term Opportunity 13

Chapter 4: How The Money Works 21

Chapter 5: A Day In The Life 29

Chapter 6: Why Selling Final Expense Is Awesome 34

Chapter 7: Why You Shouldn't Sell Final Expense 39

Chapter 8: How To Get Started 46

Chapter 9: Become Ready To Sell Within 14 Days 57

Chapter 10: Final Expense Lead Generation 101 63

Chapter 11: Final Expense Telesales Script Review 68

Chapter 12: The Blueprint For Success 85

Appendix: FAQ 87

Appendix: Glossary 89

Introduction: Welcome to Final Expense Telesales

Congratulations on taking the first step to a rewarding career! By reading this book, you are one step closer to a fulfilling and lucrative career, working from home closer to your family. If you have a strong work ethic, if you are committed to learning and growth, and you like to work in partnership with high performing people, then final expense telesales is for you.

This book will give you the A to Z on everything that it takes to be successful selling final expense insurance over the phone. I will cover the basics of final expense, what you need to know to get started, and share my script that our agents use to sell a million dollars of annualized premium in new business every single month.

Here's what this book will cover:

The Basics Of Final Expense Telesales And Why We Love It

If you've got this book, I assume that you may not know much about final expense telesales. So I will start off by introducing the concept and the business and the foundation of what you need to understand the business and how to get involved.

Short- And Long-Term Opportunity

After the basics, I want to share what makes final expense telesales different from other sales opportunities. I'll go through both the short-term and long-term opportunities that make final expense telesales a great opportunity, not just right now, but over the next 20 years. Final expense is one of the safest business models to be in relative to others that are out there, and it's here to stay.

How The Money Works Selling Final Expense

I'm sure one of your biggest questions about selling final expense is: How do I make money? This chapter will go through all the details of the money and costs and expenses.

A Day In The Life Of A Final Expense Telesales Agent

Many agents who are new to the business wonder how the process actually works. How do you actually sell? What does the day look like? This chapter will go in detail about what the day in the life of a final expense telesales agent looks like.

16 Reasons Why Selling Final Expense Remotely Is Awesome

I'm not going to try to hide it: I think selling final expense through telesales is awesome. And I have 16 reasons to prove it. We have shifted our business model at The DIG Agency to focus almost completely on this model - in this chapter, I'll share why.

Straight Talk: Why Selling Final Expense May NOT Be A Good Idea

Even though I think final expense telesales is awesome, it's not for everyone. I don't want to say anyone can do it and be successful. Not everyone can! So I want to show you the other side of the coin and talk about the drawbacks to the model. I don't want you to waste your time or money if this business model isn't a good fit for you.

Steps To Getting Started On The Right Foot

Assuming that you have decided this is for you, I'm going to share the steps to getting started on the right foot, from the pre-licensing to licensing process, and then talk about some strategic decisions you need to make as a new agent. This chapter will cover things like how to pick the right agency, how to handle leads, and much more.

What Top Producers Do To Become Sales Ready Within 14 Days

With those strategic considerations covered, I'll move on to the nitty gritty of what you need to do in the first 14 days of your career as a final expense telesales agent. I've surveyed my top producers at the DIG Agency about what they did to prepare before they got on the phone and started selling, and I'll share what I heard in this chapter.

Final Expense Lead Generation 101

We'll get into the specifics of lead generation, what leads are good, what leads are bad, and what leads you should stay away from. This is a critical chapter because leads are the lifeblood of your business as a final expense telesales agent.

Reviewing Our $1,000,000 Annualized Premium Per Month Final Expense Telesales Script

My agency is literally selling well over a million dollars in annualized premium sales every single month using the script that I'll share with you in this book. This is the exact script we use and I'm going to share it with you, for free. I like to give stuff away, what can I say? If you follow this script, you know it back-to-front, and you practice it over and over, you *will* see success at final expense telesales.

Putting It All Together: The Blueprint For Success

I'll share some final thoughts on how to create your blueprint for success in this business.

That's it! Once you finish this book, you will be ready to take on the challenge of selling final expense over the phone and dramatically change your lifestyle and career. Let's get started.

Chapter 1: My Story

Before we get into the meat of the book, I want to take a few moments to tell you about my career arc in the final expense business. Mine is a story of both failure and success.

Before Final Expense - My First Entrepreneurial Endeavor

In 2006, after graduating Boston University, I was full of hope and ambition. I had just lost a bunch of weight and decided to open my own personal training gym. I wanted to avoid the corporate grind at all costs. For a few years, it seemed like I had it all figured out. But then the Great Recession hit, and suddenly, everything changed. In just one month, I lost a third of my clients, and the gym I had worked so hard to build started sinking fast. By 2009, it was obvious I was just trying to stay afloat until I could find a lifeline.

Desperation was creeping in. I needed to do something, anything, to pull myself out of the financial hole I was quickly falling into. I started looking at corporate jobs, even though the idea of going down that path still didn't appeal to me. But then, while scrolling online, I stumbled upon something unexpected: final expense insurance.

Discovering Final Expense Sales

At first, I didn't know much about insurance, let alone final expense insurance. Despite not being familiar with the product, I started digging. I ended up on an insurance forum where agents were talking about how final expense was activity-driven—just about seeing people and closing sales. I liked that. I didn't want to deal with complex products like annuities or Medicare, which would take months to understand and even longer to make a real income from. I needed quick money, and final expense insurance seemed to be the answer.

I dipped my toes in cautiously, still keeping my gym open in case things didn't work out. But within my first few months, I started doing well. I wrote $6,000 in annualized premium in my first month, and by the sixth month, I was selling $15,000 to $20,000 in annualized premium a month. That's when I decided to close the gym and go all-in on insurance. It felt like the right decision, but soon, I learned how much damage I could do to myself when I overthink things.

I'm a marketer at heart, and after a while, working with the same old direct mail leads felt boring to me. I wanted something more efficient, something fresh, and so I decided to create my own leads. I poured $3,000 into untested marketing—money I couldn't afford to lose. And, unfortunately, it didn't pan out.

My Lowest Point

It was a hard pill to swallow when, in June of that year, I checked my balance and saw $95 staring back at me. I was $50,000 in credit card debt from the failed gym, with a wife and a child depending on me. To make matters worse, I had to admit to my wife that she had been right all along: I should've gotten a stable job instead of chasing a dream that wasn't working out.

The final straw came during a sales call. I had been chasing down leads all day, and this one appointment seemed like my last hope. I broke one of my own rules and called to confirm the meeting. The lady on the other end told me she had just bought a policy from someone else. I was devastated. Her son had set the appointment, and I had thought I had a real shot. But her words stung, and that was it—I quit the business.

The Aftermath (And Recovery)

I took a job at a uniform services company. It was the first "real" job I had ever had. I come from a family of entrepreneurs—my father, my grandfather—so it was in my blood to build something of my own. But I needed that job, and more importantly, I needed that failure. Working at the uniform services company taught me what it felt like to have no control over my own destiny, to have to wait for promotions and take orders from people who didn't know half of what I did. It showed me what I was giving up by walking away from my own business.

After a few months, I had a wake-up call. The real reason I failed wasn't because of the insurance business—it was because of me. My ego had gotten in the way. I was trying to reinvent the wheel instead of sticking to the fundamentals that had worked for years in final expense insurance. I made a decision: I was getting back in.

When I returned to the final expense business, I did things differently. I worked hard—really hard—until 11pm most nights, while my wife, pregnant with twins, supported me from home. I stuck to the basics, using direct mail leads like I had in the beginning, and I followed the system. It wasn't glamorous, but it worked. Slowly but surely, my business began to thrive again. After a year of juggling part-time final expense sales and my full-time uniform services job, I quit my job, went full-time into final expense, and never looked back!

From Agent To Agency Owner

By 2013, I realized that if I wanted to truly build something bigger than myself, I needed to pivot. I had two options: either dive into Medicare or start building an agency to teach other agents how to avoid the mistakes I had made. Looking at the landscape, I saw a need for quality training in final expense. Most agents were getting caught in the same multi-level marketing traps I had fallen into early on, and no one was teaching them how to really succeed.

So, I pivoted. I focused on training agents, building my agency, and helping others find the same success I had found after my rough start. As of 2024, we've recruited over 5,000 agents, sell $1,300,000 to $2,000,000 in new final expense premium monthly, and our entire operation is focused on training agents to sell final expense remotely from the comfort of their home. Additionally, we've built a popular insurance sales and marketing training YouTube channel (The DIG Agency!), averaging 100,000 views monthly with over 46,000 subscribers, and have more than 9,700 members in our free Insurance Sales Success forum.

Now that you know a little more about me, let's get you started on learning the fundamentals of successfully selling final expense remotely, over the phone!

Chapter 2: The Basics Of Final Expense Telesales And Why We Love It

I'm not going to presume that you know much about the final expense business. I want to be as comprehensive as possible. For some of you, some of what I include in this chapter is going to be repetitive. That's ok - if there's something you already know, go ahead and skip it. The goal with this book is to give you all the tools you need to succeed at final expense telesales.

What Is Final Expense Life Insurance?

In service of giving you everything you need, I'm going to start at the beginning: What is final expense insurance?

The answer is pretty simple: Final expense is life insurance to cover burial and cremation costs.

Easy, right? Well, usually when you tell someone this, they have a lot of questions. Such as: does the plan pay out to the funeral home? This is the question I get the most.

And here's the answer: No. The way a final expense plan works is very simple. When the insured person, that's the person that has the policy, dies, then the beneficiary, or the person who gets the money when that person dies, can do whatever they want with it.

I always used to joke with my clients, saying: "Hey, you can get this policy on yourself and give it to your kid and they can do whatever they want with it. If they want to blow the money and go on a trip to Hawaii and put you up in the morgue and keep you on ice for a while, well, that's fine!" And that's true, technically. Most of the time kids love their parents enough to put them away properly.

Its purpose is no different than life insurance that is used to pay for anything related to end-of-life expenses, such as the funeral cost, the cemetery cost, the cremation, or any other last bills. That's why we call it final expense - because that is all encompassing of any end-of-life final expenses.

The Ultimate Salesperson's Product

The unique qualities of final expense products make it the ultimate salesman's product. It's quick to get approvals thus quick to sell, and it's a simple sales process. Agents new to the business can complete a presentation and approve an application in under an hour.

There are four main reasons that make final expense unique as the ultimate salesperson's product:

1. No medical exams are necessary;
2. You can get an instant decision on the first sales call;
3. There's flexible underwriting; and
4. Small coverage amounts.

Easy Approval Process - No Medical Exams

First of all, final expense is a simplified issue product. This means that you don't have to go through a rigorous medical exam. You do not have to take blood, pee in a cup or any of those things that you would find normally with other forms of insurance. Instead, at the presentation, when you sit down with your final expense prospect, all you have to do is make a phone call or submit an application to get an underwriting decision.

Sometimes you, as the salesperson, don't even have to talk to anybody. You submit the application electronically and it pulls health information from the Medical Information Bureau as well as a prescription check service to review prescribed medication history. This information helps determine what's called "insurability," which means the ability for the client to get qualified for insurance coverage.

Instant Underwriting Decisions

This leads to the second reason why final expense is so great: it's customary to get instant decisions before the sales presentation ends.

Why does this matter? These days, clients and prospects want answers immediately. And with a final expense product featuring an instant underwriting decision, that's what they get without the weeks or months it takes to get approved with a fully underwritten life insurance application. From the standpoint of maximizing your presentation sales numbers, the final expense agent can close more new business on average, leading to potentially higher income.

Flexible Underwriting

Finally, final expense products offer flexible underwriting. This is a big difference from fully underwritten life insurance products. Because final expense is a simplified issue product, it tends to afford more flexible underwriting than what you would find with a nonmedical or a fully underwritten type of plan that has more stringent underwriting.

This is great because a lot of our clients in the final expense business are older. They typically are on Social Security, they're retired or disabled, and they come with a litany of health problems and a full box of prescription medications. In other words, due to their myriad of health issues, they are harder to qualify for life insurance coverage!

Here's the good news: this is not the case with final expense, as many final expense products offer quality coverage to otherwise uninsurable people. In fact, some final expense carriers offer "guaranteed issue" coverage, insuring anyone no matter how bad their health is, so long as their age falls within the acceptable ranges.

Small Coverage Amounts

One final benefit of final expense is that these plans have smaller amounts of coverage. This might not seem like a big deal, but it matters when considering the smaller costs of final expenses. For example, the full cost of being cremated ranges between $1,000 to $5,000. A burial can be $7,000 to $25,000, depending on the type of casket, or mausoleum versus in-ground burial. The policy sizes are designed around making sure that those policy amounts are covered for what the client needs and nothing more. Because these are smaller amounts, again, it's easier to get approved and clients on board.

Now that you understand the basics of final expense life insurance and why it's a simple sale, we'll now move on to discussing the short-term and long-term career opportunity the final expense business provides new agents.

Chapter 3: Short- and Long-Term Opportunity

If you're new or thinking about getting into the insurance sales business, you might be thinking about selling products other than life insurance, like Medicare or health insurance policies. While there is opportunity in either niche, I believe specializing in selling final expense is where the money's at.

Let's discuss those short- and long-term reasons why selling final expense remotely can offer a lucrative career in insurance sales.

Quick To Learn

What does selling final expense offer you in the short-term? First, remote final expense sales is not overly technical, making it simple to get the hang of. If you're a newly licensed agent, this is very helpful if you want to get up and running quickly. Between memorizing the sales script and carrier application process, it only takes a couple of days for the new agent to learn. Then, once you're comfortable performing the script and navigating the final expense product options for your future clients, all that's left is to get on the phone and start selling!

Easy Licensing Process

In order to sell final expense insurance, all you need is a life insurance license. While there's lots of material to learn, the test is not difficult to pass. Most states require a 70% or better to pass and qualify for your life insurance license. If you're disciplined and can focus on studying the pre-exam material for two hours every day, you should be ready to take the test within two weeks.

A True "Rinse & Repeat" Sales Process

Another advantage of selling final expense remotely: the sales process is simple. Do you like the idea of repetitively performing the same task with little variation? If so, then you'll love selling final expense. While no two clients are the same, there's little variation in executing the sales presentation and qualifying clients for coverage.

However, simplicity has its drawbacks. For some, selling remotely and rarely leaving home will drive some people nuts! And agents with a creative side may struggle with boredom. If that's you, my advice is to find a hobby outside of final expense telesales to keep your brain occupied. For me, doing jiu jitsu several times a week was the trick to keep away the boredom!

Minimal Financial Investment

Another immediate advantage of selling final expense: there's little financial investment to begin with. Depending on your home state, getting licensed costs between $200 and $400. You'll need to pay for professional liability coverage called errors and omissions, which costs $40 a month.

Beyond licensing and professional liability, the only other cost is leads. Leads are people who express interest in buying final expenses insurance. Some agents pay $1000 or more every week to have enough leads to sell to, while others join agencies that cover the cost of leads entirely, like my agency. So, if paying $50,000 or more yearly sounds scary, don't worry. You don't have to take on this expense. There are agencies designed to cover that expense entirely for you.

Remote-Friendly Sales Model

Selling final expense is remote-friendly. With COVID forcing the shutdown of the traditional face-to-face business model, carriers and agents adapted to a largely remote sales process. Also, with remote work in high demand, new agents now expect the sales process to require no in-person visits. Thankfully, many final expense carriers allow agents to sell remotely, anywhere in the nation, as long as you are licensed in the state your client lives in. Many final expense insurance companies now allow you to work internationally, too.

Telesales, Not Zoom

Since final expense prospects are elderly, agents commonly use the telephone, not Zoom meetings, to conduct sales presentations. However, as comfort with technology improves over the next decade-plus, we expect to see more remote agents use Zoom presentations.

Long-Term Opportunity

Let's shift gears and talk about the long-term opportunity selling final expense remotely provides.

As we have seen with COVID, elections, and economic changes, many business models and industries are in flux. The only constant is change! And for many, change is not good for business. Think about the downside of the housing crisis in 2009. Would you want to begin a career selling real estate back then? Of course not.

Here's my point: it's imperative to pick an industry where the trend is not against you, and the long-term opportunity is fundamentally sound. Luckily, that is the situation we find ourselves in regarding selling final expense. The business model is strong in a variety of ways.

Growing Population Of Prospects

The strongest foundational strength to selling final expense is the growing population of elderly people in America. Through the 2020s into the 2040s, an average of 10,000 to 11,000 people turn 65 *each day*. Further, people 65 and older will jump from 11% of the population today to 17% of the population by the 2050s.

Why should you care? First, more elderly people means more prospects for final expense policies. Simply put, you think about dying more as you age, thus preparing financially for funeral expenses. They've had loved ones die. They've seen how expensive it is to get buried and they're going to be top of mind about this product because of that age.

Zero History Of Government Intervention

Another advantage of selling final expense is that there's no history of government intervention into the final expense market as there has been with other insurance products.

The most recent example of government messing with a business model was the passage of the Affordable Healthcare Act in the early 2010s. Before the government intervened into health insurance, agents could sell individual health insurance plans and earn a residual lifetime income. As the health insurance carriers adapted their business to the new government mandates, they reduced and eventually eliminated commissions paid to agents. Health insurance agents with significant renewal income lost all of it in the span of a few years.

You may support government intervention in healthcare. You may not. Frankly, your politics doesn't matter to me. What DOES matter is the impact of how government legislation can upend your business. And my point is this: recognizing this reality and how it affects your future income is vital when selecting an insurance niche specialty.

The good news is that the final expense industry has no history or evidence of future government-intervention. To date, beyond customary state-based regulatory measures, there has been no federal move to intervene or alter the final expense market.

Our Clients Receive A Guaranteed Income

Did you know that the majority of final expense clients are retired and/or disabled, living on Social Security or Disability income? These federally-mandated and protected social safety nets provide one of the strongest reasons why it's intelligent for agents to specialize in final expense. In short, final expense clients are all receiving a guaranteed, government-promised income that has little risk of future alteration.

Altering Social Security is the third rail of politics. In other words, no politician wants to seriously change Social Security for fear of losing his political office.

Because our clients have a guaranteed income that no political figure truly wants to eliminate, chances are strong that you can depend on your final expense clients to always have the money on hand to pay their premiums. This means a bad economy impacts our clients less compared to younger prospects who must work to earn a living, and may cancel his life insurance coverage to save money in bad times.

First-Hand Experience With Death & Funerals

Another fundamentally sound reality is that almost all of our clients have first-hand experience with death, and thus are more open to buying final expense coverage. Unlike younger people who think dying happens to other, older people, our prospects "get it" - you do not have to hard sell final expense prospects. They understand the need for coverage. Rest assured, your clients have thought about death because they've experienced death! Death of their spouses, the death of their friends, families, and co-workers. Death has made our clients aware that life is fragile and will inevitably end, and that a huge bill waits for their loved ones at their demise.

These are the fundamental reasons why final expense is such a good short-term *and* long-term opportunity. Now, let's shift gears and discuss the money behind selling final expense remotely.

Chapter 4: How The Money Works Selling Final Expense

How does the money work when selling final expense?

Glad you asked!

You'll be happy to know that how you earn money is pretty simple. Here is the the calculation:

Your Revenue (Commissionable Earnings) Minus Your Expenses (Leads, Licensing, etc.) Equals Your Profit

Told you it was simple =).

Now, let's go into more detail so you better understand how to arrive at what you could potentially earn selling final expense.

Revenue

In short, revenue equals the commissions you earn from each sale. And the commissions you earn from each sale is based on what's known as the annual premium multiplied by your product's commission percentage, meaning:

Revenue = Annual Premium x Commission Percentage

First, let's calculate a hypothetical annual premium. Take your monthly final expense premium and multiply it by 12. Let's imagine the premium is $100 a month. So, multiply $100 by 12 and you get a $1200 annual premium.

Next, take the $1,200 annual premium and multiply it by 40% (our hypothetical commission percentage). That gives you $480 in total revenue.

Expenses

Now we've derived revenue, let's talk about expenses. Expenses are anything that you need to pay for to be in business. Leads are the biggest cost. It's typical for final expense agents to spend $750 to $1,000 a week to generate leads. (Of course, there are agencies like mine where you do not have to pay for leads since they are free! But that will lead to a lower commission, which I'll explain more below.)

In addition to leads, you'll also have other expenses:

- **A CRM to organize your data and your leads.** That's about $100 to $150 a month, but again, depending on your agency, they may offer that to you for free.

- **A dialer to help you make your costs.** That's around $150-$200 a month, unless your agency offers that technology to its agents at no cost.
- **Pricing and underwriting software.** This runs around $30 to $40 a month. We like InsuranceToolKits.com and BestPlanPro.com.
- **Licensing fees, which are about $200 to $400.** If you are selling over the phone, you will likely sell out of state, and so you need a license in each state that you sell to. For example, at The DIG Agency, we make our agents buy additional licenses, which can drive licensing costs beyond $1000.
- **Finally, you need errors and omissions insurance** (also known as professional liability insurance), which costs approximately $40 a month.

So here's what that all comes down to, in terms of a monthly and one-time costs (I'll use the more expensive end of the estimate just to be more conservative in the costs):

Profit

All of those costs may seem like a lot, but what matters is the profit left over after expenses. For agents getting leads at no cost, the goal is to generate $250 to $300 profit per sale on average.

Buying your own leads? You would want to see around $400 to $600 in profit per case. That may seem counterintuitive - you have more expenses, so you make more profit? Yes, *if* you can generate high quality leads affordably.

Renewals

Now, if you have experience in insurance, you may be thinking about the profit on renewals. Renewals are the income you receive after the first year of the policy completes. Unfortunately, renewals are not a significant source of income in final expense. If there are renewals paid, they are so low that they really won't make that much of a difference on your bottom line.

What Commission Rate Is Considered "Good?"

A good commission rate depends on a number of factors. For example, if you have to pay for leads, a 40% commission is terrible and will yield little if any profit after paying for marketing costs. However, 40% is a fair commission rate if leads are provided for free with the agency handling marketing costs.

Unfortunately, it's not always that simple, but I can give you some general advice, no matter your situation. As a rule of thumb, if you're buying leads, expect commission levels at a minimum of 80% to 90%. Any less than that, you'll likely make little to no money after lead costs. With free leads, a commission of 30% or more is fair as long as lead and training quality is solid.

Advance Commissions

Another "cost" to consider is your advance rate. Unfortunately, some of your policies are going to lapse, which means you won't necessarily receive your full annual premium on a policy. This reduces your revenue.

Let me go back to that original example. While you can plan for $600 in first year commission on a single sale, this isn't actually earned. The money is an advance payment. "Advance" is another term for a loan. You are getting loaned a percentage of the future revenue as your commission payment. If the policy lapses before the advance is cleared through enough payments, you may owe a percentage of that advance back. Most final expense carriers pay a 75% advance rate, and agents are on the hook for up to 9 months to repay.

So in this example, you are actually only getting $450, or 75% of the $600 commission.

Pay On Issue Versus Pay On First Payment

Sometimes you get "paid on issue" shortly after the policy is approved, or you get paid only after the first premium payment processes. Typically, "pay on issue" means you get paid a couple of days after the policy is approved, but before the first payment comes in. Pay on first payment means the policy's approved, then it is issued, but you don't get paid until the payment occurs. And most final expense is sold "buy now, pay later," meaning getting paid after the first payment happens weeks after the policy is approved. Obviously, you want to have pay on issue, which is faster than pay on first payment.

Paid Versus Free Leads

With all of that discussion about profit and expenses, you may be wondering which route you should go: Should I buy leads or get leads from my agency for free? My opinion:

for 90% of people looking to get into this business, you should do a free lead program.

I came to this conclusion recruiting agents to buy their own leads for more than 10 years. In 2023 we started our free lead telesales program for final expense, and my entire perspective changed. When agents join a free lead program, they're more emotionally and mentally resilient, and more consistent in their sales results compared to agents buying their own leads, who experience more mental instability, and are frequently more frustrated, and less successful making sales.

Why? I think it's because of the risk associated with investing money. For example if a new agent spends $1,000 a week on leads, while he'll have some good weeks, he'll also have bad ones, too.

With this kind of volatility, with so much more money in expenses going out the door, you start to get scared. You start making bad decisions about your business at the exact moment you need to just stick with a plan and move through the ups and downs.

Even though we can train agents on how to think in this situation, there's an emotional component when it comes to your money being at risk that causes all sorts of unintended consequences. This is why I think the free lead program is superior. Why? First, you start at zero every week instead of negative. It sounds simple, but I can't stress enough how powerful that is for the vast majority of people. All you have to worry about is just picking up the phone and dialing and closing and not worrying about spending the money to buy leads.

However, you may be an entrepreneur, somebody who's run businesses, and you know what that takes and what it means. You may be better off as an agent buying his or her own leads.

For example, I'm an entrepreneur. I probably would never do a free lead program. But not everyone is, and that's why I don't recommend buying leads to most people.

Bottom line, most agents new to final expense should seriously consider a free lead program to minimize their financial risk while also optimizing their sales capability.

Chapter 5: A Day In The Life Of A Final Expense Telesales Agent

I hope I've convinced you now why selling final expense over the phone is a great option for you. I've covered the fundamentals, the opportunities, and the money.

But maybe you need a little more information about what your day-to-day life looks like. If so, let me break it down for you in this chapter.

Starting Your Day

I always recommend agents to start their days at 7:00 AM or 8 AM. This depends on where you live, of course. If you live in California, you could start at 5:00 in the morning because the East Coast will be up, and you can start dialing for there. Wherever you live, though, you want to start your day early.

Review Pending Cases & Missed Payments

When you start your day, my recommendation is always to review your cases on your carrier website before you start to call. Do a report on where things stand so that you can reach out to anyone with lapsed payments or missed payments, in order to ask them what's going on. You can also check on approvals, but since most of the policies are approved on the first call, it's less about approval status, and more about just policy retention.

With this information, schedule follow-ups with any clients that you need to help.

This pre-call work may take about 30 minutes on average. Some days require more than others. But there's very little service work in the final expense business, which is a strong benefit of this product. You want to sell, not spend time dealing with client management!

Sunrise To Sunset: Dial, Dial, Dial!

Once this is done, you start your calls. Your goal, is to close the sale on the first call. What you don't want is to start your calls and think that you are going to do anything other than closing sales. In other words, what you don't want to allow the lead to say: "Call me back later," or "I can't talk right now."

Do exceptions happen? Sure, but they're exceptions, not rules. The rule is that you must sell on the first call.

It's Simple, Not Easy

So is final expense telesales really that simple? Just make calls and that's it?

Well, no! The truth is about calling anyone these days is this: It's tough to get them to pick up the phone!

Here's the truth: it's going to take a lot of calls to get people to actually pick up the phone.

Tips To Get Your Prospects To Pick Up The Phone

There are a few strategies that can help get people on the phone:

- **Triple Dialing:** Triple dialing involves you calling your prospect three times in a row over a short period of time. Calling three times is usually what it takes to get people to pick up the phone that otherwise never would, and allows you to connect with more of your leads.
- **Use A Quality Dialer:** Forget using your personal phone. It'll likely get flagged as spam or a telemarketer, greatly diminishing your pick-up rates. Instead, use a professional dialer like Kixie that provides you scrubbed phone numbers to avoid the "spam likely" carrier filters.

- **Follow The Script**: When you reach a prospect, present according to the script. Keep in mind: it's imperative that you don't "wing" your calls, or that you follow only part of the script. When you're selling, have your script up in front of you on the monitor, reading it as you are presenting, until you have memorized the thing. Even when you've memorized it, you probably should have it up anyway.

If you follow the script consistently and have great work ethic, set a goal for yourself of selling one in every four leads you speak with on the phone. This means for every four lead contacts you make, and you go through the whole script presentation, you should expect one sale.

Breaks

Because this work is so task-focused, I recommend taking breaks throughout the day to regroup and then get back on the phone. Selling final expense remotely is a performance-based activity. Being a salesperson is like being a professional athlete; all the same things that affect an athlete affect you: your mental state, your emotional state, your ability to focus. It's important to not just work and grind it out constantly all day, but to also take some rest periods.

End Of Day

The nicest thing about telesales is that when you are done, you're at home. When I'm done with my day, I leave my home office, I'm with my wife, my four kids, and I can have dinner with them.

As a telesales agent, you have such a blessing that the face-to-face agent doesn't have. A face-to-face agent must travel sometimes hours away to speak to a prospect. Thankfully, this will not be your life as a remote agent: You are right there with your family at the end of the day, even when you work late.

Expect To Work Late Sometimes

I do recommend that you sell from 5PM to 9PM on several of your working days. If you don't call much beyond 5 PM at any point throughout the week, you're missing sales. Which means you're not going to make as much money as you'd like.

Chapter 6: 16 Reasons Why Selling Final Expense Remotely Is Awesome

You've read about the fundamentals, you've read about the money, and you've read about what your day will look like. If you need any more reasons to get on board, I've compiled the 16 high points of what makes final expense so great to sell.

1. **No Sex Appeal**. Having no sex appeal may be surprising to you as a "benefit." Most think of it as a detriment! But it's true: almost no one grows up wanting to sell final expense life insurance. In fact, there are professional life insurance agents that look down on burial insurance, thinking it's beneath them. They sell "real" insurance. And it's that attitude that makes final expense attractive as it makes it a less competitive niche compared to the "hot" insurance niches. And less competition means more opportunity to make money.

2. **One-Call Close**. You're going to make money faster selling final expense than selling other insurance products, because it is a one-call-close business model.

3. **Fast Pay**. When you make a sale, you're going to get

paid within days to weeks. You're making a commission quickly, relative to fully underwritten products and annuities, which can take months to move through compliance and underwriting.

4. **Solid First-Year Commission**. Depending if you are buying your leads or not, you'll earn an average of $300-600 in commission per final expense policy sale. Even better, if you like working hard and want to make more money, you can scale up your business and start selling 5, 10, 20 or more policies weekly.

5. **Easy To Get Leads**. There's multiple platforms where you can find leads. For example, Facebook is what we use at The DIG Agency, because that's where the old people are nowadays. But that's not the only option: We also use TikTok for leads, because many grandparents are on TikTok to connect with their grandkids. Agents also love television commercial-generated leads, too.

6. **Simple Sales Process**. Final expense is easy to understand as a new agent, and it's easy for the client to understand. It shouldn't take you more than a week to two studying your carrier and sales training material to be sales ready.

7. **Favors Remote Sales**. Because of COVID and the lockdowns in the early 2020s, all the carriers shifted to accommodating remote based final expense agents.

8. **Growing Base of Prospects**. Ten thousand to eleven thousand Baby Boomers are turning 65 daily well into the 2040s. We're going to see a 50% increase in the population over 65 from 2020 to 2040. And all of this means one thing: more people to sell to!

9. **Guaranteed Income**. Over 90% of our final expense prospects are retired and receiving a guaranteed Social Security or Disability based income. A guaranteed income means more certainty that our clients have the money to pay their premiums.

10. **Simple To Scale**. Want to make more money selling final expense? Just do more work!

11. **Cross-Selling Opportunities**. You can cross-sell other products beyond final expense to your final expense leads. I don't recommend that you do this until you're a year into the business. Some agents are just fine doing final expense strictly, but if you want to cross-sell, there are opportunities to do so with products like Medicare policies,

annuities, and ACA health insurance.

12. **Agency-Building Opportunities**. If you get good and want to scale your work through building an agency, you can definitely do so. I know from experience!

13. **The Ability to Shop for Your Clients**. As a final expense agent, you can choose to join an agency that has access to many different carriers. This means you can shop and find the best combination of price and coverage for our clients, which may lead to more of your clients keeping your policy instead of dropping it.

14. **No Government Intervention**. There's no history of government intervention in final expense, as compared to health insurance and Medicare. This means less chance for disruption of your business due to government policy shifts or election cycles.

15. **Does Not Require Much Intelligence**. Don't worry, I'm not insulting you! But truth be told, sometimes having "a big brain" gets in the way of being successful. If you overthink this otherwise simple business, you may simply think your way out of the business. The good news is that you don't need a genius level IQ to do well. Final expense is

a rinse and repeat business model. Avoid reinventing the wheel. Just follow the system if you want to see success!

16. No Inventory. You don't have to buy equipment or raw goods like in other industries to create your product. In final expense, the policy is made when the sale is made, allowing you to not have financial skin in the game to create a policy and make a profit.

Chapter 7: Why Selling Final Expense May NOT Be A Good Idea

Now that I've shared with you all the amazing reasons why you should get into final expense, I'm going to tell you why you may NOT be a good fit for final expense remote sales. I'm including this as a chapter because an agent gave me some straight talk. He said: "Look Dave, you can't talk about the rainbows and sunshine and how great this business is without talking about the raw truth. Because some of it's bad."

I considered this and thought, "You know what? He's right."

The truth is there's good and bad in any business model. I don't want to hide this from you - my goal is for you to have all the information you need to get into the final expense business, which must include information about how it can be hard. You need to carefully consider if the realities of this business are a good fit for your personality type. If it's not, then don't do it. There are plenty of other opportunities out there.

Final Expense Is Work. A LOT of Work

First, let's talk about the failure rate. Around 90% to 95% of new life insurance agents fail out within their first year as an agent. That's pretty bad. And part of the reason why many people fail out is they don't take this career as seriously as they should.

For example, when you start, you have to ask yourself: what do you really want out of this business? For most, they want something that's easy to make them a lot of money. They don't want to work hard but still want to make great money.

That's not the final expense remote business! Final expense takes lots of work, and lots of commitment. You have to ask yourself: Can you really put in 40 to 50 plus hours a week consistently doing the job? If you can't - unless you are really dialed in on a part-time basis - this is not for you.

Here's what I'm trying to convey: Don't jump into final expense sales because I've told you how awesome it is and how you can make a lot of money. You can accomplish these goals, but it comes with a Herculean level of work and effort.

Lack Of Training

Another big reason why people fail is because they just aren't trained well. Mentorship and training is critical to your success as a final expense remote agent.

Think of yourself as an apprentice. You must learn from "the master." You must have that mindset coming into this business. Time and time again, I've seen poor-performing agents become top producers in a matter of months, because they found a mentor that showed them how to improve while keeping them accountable.

Many insurance sales models - especially the Multi-Level Marketing models - don't care about training and mentorship opportunities, because they are not that interested in selling. They only want to recruit and make money off of bringing in new people, or by monetizing your contacts without returning anything to the agent. If you are in a situation where you aren't getting the training you need, consider leaving as soon as possible and finding an agency interested in training and developing you.

No Lead Generation

In final expense, leads are the lifeblood of your business. If you don't have leads or prospects, you don't have a final expense tele-sales business. You have already failed before you know it.

When joining an agency, make sure they have a turnkey system that puts you in front of good prospects. In our free lead program, we have developed a phenomenal system to generate high quality prospects and leads for our agents. So all our agents have to do is pick up the phone and dial and close.

Before joining an agency, ask: How is their approach to generating leads? If they can't give you an answer, then move on.

Entrepreneurial Shock

Entrepreneurial shock is the realization that the fantasy and the allure of entrepreneurship imposed upon social media is not reality.

When you're an entrepreneur, you don't really have freedom. If you want to make money, you're going to be working your tail off for hours and hours on end, and there's no guarantee that you'll see any success.

There's also income inconsistency. If you've been on a paycheck your whole life and you move into a role where you're on a straight commission, it's a shock. It changes your behaviors that you otherwise wouldn't have if you knew there was a guarantee on your income. You can't spend every dollar you get. There's no guarantee you're going to make any more money tomorrow. You need to be padding your bank account for the down periods.

Taxes are another big concern that hits agents. You have way more you need to pay than you did before - you have to pay not only quarterly taxes, but also the other half of payroll tax and Social Security that your former employer paid.

Chargebacks

Chargebacks can be another big issue. Chargebacks are the monies that you were paid that you must repay because your client lapsed before the advance debt covered it. As soon as a policy lapses, if the advance hasn't been covered by the premiums the client has paid, then you owe back whatever portion hasn't been paid.

Chargebacks go up when agents oversell. All that does is cause what you had earned to now be a debt that you have to pay back.

Boredom

Remember how I said earlier that final expense is a simple business? If you are a creative type of personality, this business becomes boring quickly. You literally will do the same thing on your first day as you will years into your career.

Sometimes, the boredom is too much and people want to branch out into things like crypto or real estate. I'm not saying those are necessarily bad, but they can become distractions. This invariably means less income and sometimes, failing out of the business.

Boredom, while a first-world problem, is a real problem. It is something to manage, and if you can't, you risk burning out.

Rejection

I'll end with the hardest thing to overcome in this business: rejection. To sell effectively, you have to handle the rejection that you will get on a daily basis. People are going to say some of the wildest, nastiest, and meanest things to you on the phone. You might as well just accept it now.

You shouldn't let that deter you personally, because rejection is not personal. But even as I teach this, and even as I explain this logically, some people just cannot handle getting put down constantly. They may follow the system, and get a couple of sales by the end of the day, but the constant rejection becomes too hard for them. It's a real issue - and if you think this might be a concern for you, you may want to reconsider going into the business.

Chapter 8: How To Get Started In Final Expense Telesales

Alright, if you weren't scared away from the last chapter, then great!

So let's keep going and talk about the steps in getting started on the right foot in this business.

Licensing

The first thing you need to sell final expense is a life insurance license. The licensing process is simple: Google search "how to get a life insurance license in your state." Then, follow the directions.

Next step is to sign up for a pre-licensing course. Pre-licensing courses require completion in virtually all states before you take the exam. I like XCEL or ExamFX. Shameless plug: You can get a discount on either when you join my free training site at davidduford.com/iss/

Pro-tip: Take the practice test several times until scoring above 80%. Then, schedule and pay for the life insurance license test with your local proctor on an in-person basis

Once you pass the life insurance exam, you'll receive guidelines on how to apply for your license. Expect to submit fingerprints, have a background check, and to pay for your license application. Total out-of-pocket costs range between $200 and $400.

Once you apply and wait a few weeks, the state Department of Insurance knights you as a bona fide life insurance agent. Welcome to the business!

Finding A Good Agency Partner

Alright, you are an official agent. So now what? Let's go through a few strategic considerations to get you off on the right foot.

First is the matter of picking an agency to join. The way to look at this is to look at it like a marriage. Hopefully, you want to be married for life. But agents don't always think that way. They don't do a good job of picking a good agency partner. If they don't make the right choice the first time, they bounce around a lot, thinking the grass is greener elsewhere. Bouncing around from agency to agency has an impact on your closing, your commissions, your carrier availability, and your production. So the best bet is to do your due diligence early on and select the best possible agency you can find.

Previous Success & References

It's not enough for an agency to claim they are the best. Newsflash - That's what EVERY agency says! My advice is to look at the agency's case studies and testimonials. For example, I have dozens of case studies and hundreds of testimonials from happy and profitable DIG Agency agents, easily viewable on my website. I want to have a preponderance of proof available to potential agents, so you can see and believe that we know what we're doing and we're a good agency to join.

You can also reach out and talk to active agents to discuss their experiences. I always tell agents to ask for three references before you join any agency. I want the potential agent to ask our current agents all about the good, bad and the ugly too, so they know what they are getting into. Because if they don't, that sets them up for failure, and I want my agents to be successful.

Transparency

You want full commission transparency in your agency partner. For example, it should be clear what your commission levels are, and what you can expect to get paid. You should know what you'll make for the products and services that you'll be writing.

You also want transparency in communications. A lot of problems, just like in a marriage, can be solved if you can just communicate with your partner. In business, if you communicate your problems early on with your agent or your agency, a lot of the problems get solved. But a lot of people that I've seen, including many agency owners, ignore problems. And ultimately, both the agency and agents suffer on some level.

Proven Lead Program

Good agencies also have a proven lead program. You only want to join an agency that has a lead program that many active agents are currently using. You don't want to be a guinea pig.

Training

You also want to see examples of excellent training, including personal mentorship. You want intensive one-on-one or group training. Also, you need foundational resources like sales scripts, underwriting guides, and opportunities for meetings and video training tutorials. You should have all of these resources, which you can review on your own or with the trainer themselves.

Fine Print

You also need to beware of the fine print in your contracts. So many agents get screwed and short handed because they don't understand the business arrangements that are unique to the insurance final expense space.

Carrier Releases

Another thing to consider is carrier release provisions. A carrier release describes how you move your carrier contracts from one agency to a different agency. There are times where your relationship with your current agency may not make sense. For example, I had an agent and he recently shifted into Medicare. My agency doesn't really focus on Medicare as much, but we've had contracts over time and he's making a strategic move to go to an agency completely focused on Medicare, not final expense.

But here's the thing: many agencies will not release your carriers. Instead, they force you to keep your carrier contracts with them until six months have passed with no production. Holding your carriers hostage after your business dealings have ceased with the agency is frustrating, and I recommend asking the agency in question their release policy before you decide to join.

Captive Versus Independent

Another thing you need to consider is being a captive agent or an independent agent. Captive agents usually have only one carrier they can work with. In contrast, an independent agent has many carriers she can choose from.

A major advantage captive agents have is an easier learning experience as a new agent. Instead of many products to learn and understand, there's just one, simplifying the onboarding process. However, simplicity for simplicity's sake isn't always superior. With only one product, you cannot offer an optimal product to your client if price or health is an issue. In some cases, captive, one-carrier only agents must "push product," knowingly selling an inferior product to unsuspecting clients.

Long-term, pushing inferior products puts you in a strategically bad position that may affect your total income. For example, selling policies with expensive pricing sets you up for future replacement, causing lapses, chargebacks, and financial frustration.

What's the solution? Consider a position as an independent agent. While selling multiple final expense products increases complexity, most agents with willpower can handle it. In exchange for the added preparation, independent agents have access to more competitively priced final expense products with flexible underwriting options. The result is the building of a proverbial moat around your client; with better prices and a better product, it's harder for other agents to replace you, meaning less chargebacks and more annual income for you!

In short, the advantages gained as an independent agent is why I went that route instead of seeking a captive position as a new final expense agent. I didn't want to push an inferior product. I wanted to offer my clients options, recognizing that better options means better quality of business. I also realized that I'll keep more of what I sell and have more sales opportunities than if I had just one product that was not a good match all the time.

Ideal Carrier Lineup

Let's look at some factors strategically you need to consider when you're looking at carriers for final expense. We talked about the one carrier versus many carriers strategy. I'm a big fan of having multiple carriers. One product is not enough to do well with this business. You'll miss out on sales, lose your clients to your competition, and arguably make much less money.

With that said, let's talk about the "must-have" elements of great final expense carriers, as not all carriers are equal in their ease-of-use as a final expense remote agent.

Telesales-Friendly Signature Process

One thing you want from a carrier is a smooth signature process. The two industry best-practices to collect signatures as a remote agent are the recorded verbal signature, or the text-to-sign option.

Verbal signing is just like it sounds. You get the client's consent to apply and accept coverage on a recorded line. This is the easiest of the two processes as there are no potentials for technological mishaps.

Text-to-sign gets the client to sign off on the application with a text confirmation. Many remote final expense agents use will utilize this process. It's easy to do and very rarely do our clients have a problem completing this process.

With that said, stay away from any signature processes that require your clients to access their email to sign. You will lose otherwise easy sales, forcing your clients to search their email to sign off on the policy.

Use Carriers With Instant-Decision Underwriting

Since final expense is a one-call close business, use carriers that provide an underwriting decision before ending the sales call. Thankfully, most carriers operate this way. So, if a client is declined for coverage, you can pivot to another carrier.

Social Security Deposit Billing Is A Must!

As much as possible, use final expense carriers that rely on Social Security deposit billing. Social Security deposit billing is when the carrier drafts your client's money on the exact date that her check hits her account. As a rule, the further out our draft is from the deposit date, the higher the chances of our carrier not collecting the money, leading to a potential lapse and chargeback.

Cross-Selling And Building An Agency

As a new agent - and perhaps as an experienced agent - I recommend staying away from cross-selling other products. I can count on one hand the number of my agents that cross-sold that are still in business today. The truth about cross-selling multiple products is that it complicates things exponentially, causing many agents to make less money. In my experience, most agents are better off selling one thing at scale to increase their income.

Finally, give careful thought to agency-building long-term. Agency building is the ultimate way to scale your income beyond your own activity. While building The DIG Agency has been great for me, there are serious drawbacks.

For example, building an agency too early distracts you from selling, resulting in short-term lower income.

Another reality is that you co-sign all of the advance debt agents create. In other words, if your agents have clients that lapse, they are responsible for paying off any chargebacks. However, if the agent doesn't pay the chargeback, the debt "rolls up" to the co-signer. That's you!

In my experience, if you are not rigorously monitoring your agents' quality of business, all it takes is a few agents writing bad business to cause you serious financial issues. Personally, I've experienced outright fraud from bad agents, resulting in hundreds of thousands in chargebacks I had to pay back out of my own pocket. But here's the upside: my agency has more than 200 actively- selling agents, which creates a lucrative income for myself and my family.

Chapter 9: How You Can Become Confident & Ready To Sell Final Expense Remotely Within 14 Days

What do you need to do to get ready to confidently sell final expense remotely? More specifically, what are the best strategies to deploy to perform at your highest level as a new final expense agent?

Role Play the Script

The most important thing before you dive into selling is to role play your sales script. With remote telesales, your success is correlated with how well you memorize and perform the sales script. And the more you practice performing the script, the better your odds are in selling policies quickly.

To role play the script, grab somebody like your friend, family member, or another new agent and practice with them. Have one of you act as the prospect, and the other as the agent. Then, switch roles and do it again, over and over. Come up with objections, work on your tonality, and ask your partner for feedback.

Record Yourself

Once you've role played a few times, start recording yourself practicing the script. Listen to your recording and critique how you sound and what you say. I promise you this: when you listen to your recordings, you'll be shocked! You'll be amazed at what scripting you messed up, and how your tonality actually sounds. And what's best is that you'll have new opportunities for improvement.

We recommend our new agents record their presentations thirty times before dialing their leads. It sounds excessive, doing so many practice runs does wonders in preparing them for the real thing.

Listen To Top Producer Sales Calls

Another thing that we recommend is reviewing top producing agents' calls. For example, new agents in my agency can listen to successful presentations given by our top agents. And when they review those calls, they can learn from real life examples of what a good opening sounds like, what good tonality is like, and how to overcome sales objections in real time. In short, becoming a top producing final expense agent requires you to emulate what other top producers do. And the best way to do that is to listen to their real-life sales presentations.

Carrier Knowledge

Once you're confident with the sales script, learn each of your final expense carriers' underwriting and application processes. Thankfully, most carriers have explainer videos that walk you through how to complete an application, and how to underwrite your clients. Make sure you spend several days reviewing these processes in advance of selling in real time. There's nothing worse than losing a sale because you do not know how to complete a carrier's application.

The Success Mindset

Preparing to sell final expense requires not only sales and carrier knowledge; you also need to have the right mindset and set realistic expectations. Let's discuss some important perspectives to develop in order to have sustainable long-term success selling final expense remotely.

Numbers Game

Final expense telesales is a numbers game. You must put in the work to get a high number of presentations if you want to sell lots of policies and make a lot of money. In other words, the inputs (time dialing, the numbers of dials and presentations) always come before the outputs (number of sales, your income). While we like talking about the financial possibilities final expense provides, the truth is before any of that happens, you must put in a significant amount of activity first.

Here's what all experienced agents discover: there's a correlation between the money you make and the amount of time you're prospecting. And what's neat is that you can get to a point where you can track those inputs and rely on them to determine your earning potential.

Build Your Sales Skill Set

Success in final expense sales is not only about activity. It's about your sales skills, too. Mindless activity without a strategy to convert mildly-interested leads into enthusiastic clients will result in failure. You must captivate and capture the client's attention, while overcoming the initial knee-jerk reaction to say "no" to a stranger on the phone. Thankfully, with the right training, you can learn the proper sales strategies to convert leads into sales.

Long-Term Perspective

A tough perspective to develop is that all successful agents face adversity through their career. Everyone wants to make big money right away. The truth is that developing yourself takes time and commitment. You have to understand and connect the realities of sticking to something long-term and overcoming the temptation to get frustrated and quit in the short term. The faster you accept this, the better off you'll be.

Be Coachable

Coachability is crucial. Do you want to do well selling final expense? Get comfortable with getting constructive criticism on every aspect of your sales presentation. Agents who accept the uncomfortableness of constructive criticism from their manager tend to get better faster.

Pro-tip: As a new agent, just do what you're told. Don't think you know better than your manager or that your ideas are inherently better. Agents who do their own thing and turn down coaching usually fail out at a rapid pace.

Summary

What success selling final expense remotely comes down to is an indomitable work ethic and humility. This business isn't that technical, doesn't take a lot of brainpower, but it does take lots of work. You're going to have to spend a lot of hours working and being on task in order to succeed. You're going to have to be good at not letting short-term failures and frustration stop your momentum. You've got to put in your time and you've got to put the inputs in if you want to see anything successful out of this business.

Chapter 10: Final Expense Lead Generation 101

Leads are the lifeblood of every final expense agent. Without leads, you do not have the capability to succeed. Therefore, understanding how leads work, and what leads are best, is critical to your success. In this chapter, I want to share my own opinions and experience on what works well for final expense lead generation.

The Fundamentals Of Leads

What is a lead? A lead is someone who has expressed an interest in your product. That's it.

Here's what a lead is not: A lead is not a guaranteed sale. Some leads turn into sales, and many of them don't. Most importantly, the ability for you to turn a lead into a sale depends mostly on your sales skill set. While a person may have interest in final expense coverage, much must be answered before buying: your lead must feel confidence about the carrier, how affordable the premium is, how your final expense plan works, and most importantly, how well they can trust you.

The reason this is important is because some agents put too much stock into lead quality, blaming their lack of results on the leads. While there are times when this is true, it usually isn't, and the true problem is the agent's lack of sales skill.

In short, it's your responsibility to take a mildly-interested lead with reservations about buying and turn her into an enthusiastic client. Never forget that!

Outbound Versus Inbound Leads

There are two different types of leads available to final expense agents: Outbound and inbound leads. Inbound leads call you, usually from television ads or online ads that ask customers to dial in for a quote. Outbound leads require you to call the lead, usually generated from an online ad.

So which is best? I prefer outbound leads. Why? Simply put, I have control over the inputs. In other words, I can control my activity and many times get more presentations completed than relying on an inbound lead system.

What's Working, And What's Not

Let's discuss strategies on lead generation that are working successfully for the final expense agent.

Internet Leads

Internet leads refers to any online platform that allows ad placement. For final expense. Social media platforms like Facebook are the most popular. That's what we do at The DIG Agency. Social media absolutely works if you've got a great ad and a great funnel process to collect that information.

TV Leads

Television-generated leads also work. These are inbound leads that come from a commercial, inviting viewers to call in to get a quote.

What Lead Sources Do Not Work For Remote Sales

Telemarketing Leads

Never buy telemarketing leads. Most are generated overseas call centers and are notorious for not following federal TCPA guidelines. And if an agent is fined or sued, there is no recourse against the call center as they fall outside of federal jurisdiction.

Direct Mail

While direct mail leads are great for traditional face-to-face final expense sales, they do not work well for remote agents. Why? Cost and lost opportunity. Leads are very expensive and take up to a month of investing your money before any are returned, and many leads do not have phone numbers listed to dial.

Buying Your Own Leads Versus Getting Free Leads?

An important decision about leads you need to make is whether or not you buy them or get them for free.

The benefit to buying leads is the possibility of a higher commission per sale. Agents buying leads carry the risk, so they should get paid more per sale.

However, after recruiting thousands of agents since 2013, I strongly believe 90% of final expense remote agents benefit the most from a free lead program.

The problem with purchasing leads is the risk of loss. In my experience, most agents struggle with simultaneously handling the emotions associated with risking money on buying leads with the mental fortitude required to sell at peak performance. Having a bad week in sales in combination with losing $1,000 on an investment in leads will lead many agents to make risky decisions about how they sell, what leads they do or do not purchase, and whether or not they follow their business plan. And as much training an agent has on overcoming this, it's extremely difficult for the vast majority to navigate successfully.

This is where the benefit of a free lead program shines through: Having no financial risk removes the pain of losing your money. Each week you start at zero as opposed to a negative number, and even if you have a bad week, you'll never lose money. All of this allows you to focus on the number one money-making activity, which is developing your sales skills and putting in the work. That's the power of a free lead final expense remote program.

Chapter 11: Reviewing Our $1,000,000/Month Final Expense Telesales Script

Now that we've discussed the nuts and bolts of the final expense remote business, let's shift gears and train you on how our final expense remote sales scripts works.

This exact script has helped my agency reliably sell $1,000,000 or more in annualized premium monthly. And you get to learn how it works, even if you never join our agency!

7 Pillars Of Success

When using our script, you need to keep our seven pillars in mind:

- <u>Pillar 1: Keep Your Prospect On The Phone:</u> You want to open strong, get to the point quickly in order to stop your prospect from hanging up.
- <u>Pillar 2: Why/Problem:</u> Make it clear early on what problem your client has that you are trying to solve. They need to know what's in it for them to continue listening.
- <u>Pillar 3: Shopping Range:</u> When applicable, give them the different price ranges available for what they qualify. Our

clients are on a fixed income and need to know what will fit their budget.

- **Pillar 4: Underwriting:** Learn how to ask the appropriate health questions to streamline the underwriting process and to eliminate rate-ups and declines.
- **Pillar 5: Introduce Yourself:** Make sure that they know who you are and they can trust you. Success depends on what you say and how you say it.
- **Pillar 6: Product Value / Differentiation:** You must succinctly explain why your final expense product is different and how it will add value to their lives and the lives of their loved ones.
- **Pillar 7: CLOSE, ask for sale, THEN do application:** Get a firm YES at the close, handle any objections, then rapidly shift to completing the application.

The Opening Of The Sales Call

> "Hey <First Name>, this is <Your Name> calling you on a recorded line with the final expense price-quote you requested on Facebook. I literally just saved a guy $43 a MONTH, it's just a few minutes, is this for yourself or a loved one? You a smoker or a non-smoker?"

<WAIT for confirmation/objection> Perfect! It's my JOB to deliver this quote over the phone about the final expense programs.

In the opening, the goal is to get to the point as quickly as possible. Our prospects are distracted, busy, and demand a clear understanding of why you're calling. Any wasted time gives them a chance to hang up or say no.

This is why we quickly identify why we're calling, mentioning which website (in this case, Facebook), that we got their information from. Additionally, we mention how much we saved for a recent client to entice them to listen longer (note: don't use the number listed above. Instead, use a number based off of a former client and how much you've saved them). Finally, we close with an easy question to answer (for yourself or a loved one?) to get them engaged and listening.

Opening Objections

Naturally, not everyone will want to listen. Prospects have objections, and it's your job to rebuttal and overcome them. Below are the two objection-rebuttals we use to overcome most objections:

Insurance Objection

<Including people who are hanging up>

<Interrupt Them RAISE VOICE>,

"GREAT that's exactly why I'm calling! Stay on the line! I literally just saved a guy $43 a MONTH, Let me do that for you as well, it's just a few minutes, are you a smoker or a non-smoker?"

All Other Objections

*"Yeah no problem, just need a few minutes to get you the pricing you wanted, and what you do with that is totally up to you, I'm not gonna try to sell you anything, just want to get you a quote, **so how long have you been looking?**"*

After the opening and any objections, we now move into Pillar 2, establishing why the client requested information and what their pain points are.

*"**How long have you been looking for a policy?**"*

Why do we ask about any existing policies in effect? First, knowing if the client has a policy is akin to playing poker with your hand face up. When we know the details of the client's policy, it makes positioning what we're selling easier. For example, if we know our client owns a policy from a company that only sells two-year waiting period policies, we can now sell the benefits of our first-day full coverage programs (assuming the client qualifies, of course). Not knowing this information about existing coverage may cost us the sale.

"Do you currently have a policy in place?"

If the client does not have coverage, we work on positioning the reasons why buying coverage today is important. For example, we discuss how much of a burden final expenses are on survivors, describing the emotional toll they'll experience. This is vital in creating the urgency necessary to persuade your prospect to purchase from you.

If they do have a policy, you can say:

"Okay, were you looking for some additional coverage or to see if you qualify for a lower monthly payment or both?"

"Perfect, well you're definitely in the right place, just last week I had a client saying the same thing, and I was able to save them $43 a month.

*Let's cut to the chase and get this done for you. **<pause>** and by the way was your policy a 2 year wait to kick in? **<wait>** and was there accidental coverage with that?" **<wait>** Got it...*

If they do NOT have a policy, you can say:

*<**amazed quieter tone**> Wow, well is there any specific reason why you haven't got something in place? (what's been holding you back from getting a policy?)*

*<**engage in whatever conversation happens here and take notes**>*

Now that you better-understand the client's final expense coverage situation, it's time to transition into qualifying the client's health:

*Okay, so let's get you the price quote here real quick. It's all based on AGE and health, so what's your Date of Birth so I can verify your AGE? **<wait>***

Remember, price quote is based on age and HEALTH so, do you have ANY mild or major health concerns of any kind?

<ask in this order and SHOW COMPASSION sincerely. We need RAPPORT here.>

- *Height/Weight Please (if you didn't already)*
- *Lung disease, COPD, Emphysema, Asthma, Oxygen, or Inhalers?*
- *Diabetic, Insulin, Kidney Insufficiency, Dialysis, or even had Cancer?*
- *Cirrhosis, Hepatitis, Heart Attack, Bypass, Stents, Pacemaker?*
- *Angina, Congestive Heart Failure*
- *Seizures, strokes, Lupus, Multiple Sclerosis?*
- *Parkinson's, Lou Gehrig's, Depression Bipolar?*
- *Schizophrenia, Alzeheimer's Dementia?*
- *Any hospitalizations overnight in the past 2 years?*
- *Drug abuse? Suboxone or narcan USE in the last 2 years?*
- *Filled a RX for Nitros in the past 2 years?*
- **Ask RXs <*from memory if they are traveling, otherwise, got a list/bottles, but do not spend too much time on this if you are going to lose the call*>**

As we begin asking questions about the prospect's health we remind them that our goal is to get the price quote to them quickly, and to do so we need to verify age and health status.

Strategically, we begin asking broad health questions like,

"Do you have any mild or major health concerns of any kind?"

before getting more specific.

For example, if a client says they have diabetes, we'll dig deeper, asking about the type of diabetes, whether or not her diabetes is insulin-dependent, and whether or not she has diabetic complications like diabetic neuropathy.

Building Rapport & Authority

Interestingly, asking health questions provides you an opportunity to build rapport and your authority. Prospects love sharing their health history and ailments, which sheds light on their life and experiences. Thoughtful agents dig into these details to better connect. Additionally, demonstrating knowledge about health issues and prescriptions builds the perception of expertise in your prospect's mind.

Introduction

After gathering your client's health history information, make sure to formally introduce yourself:

By the way, if you missed it my name is <YOUR NAME>. Obviously I am a licensed broker here in <THEIR STATE>. I shop all the 30+ major insurance companies, and get you qualified for the LOWEST monthly price. LOWEST monthly price is my absolute obsession FOR YOU, sound good?

I love his introductory statement because it explains to your prospect who you are, why you're calling, and why people do business with you. As in the underwriting section, a proper introduction further builds rapport and authority with your prospect.

Collecting Payment Information

Now that you've introduced yourself, let's shift gears and collect payment information from the client as follows:

Some carriers take certain payment methods, others do not, so do you have a valid US bank account? <wait if no, what type of payment card. If not viable payment, hangup and #GFM>

<FIRST NAME> everyone I work with is on a fixed income, so the goal is to find something that you can qualify for and also afford. <wait>

They have the programs sorted in different price ranges, so I need you to tell me what range to start shopping in. <short pause while thinking> OH WOW, I imagine you don't want this crazy policy at $400 a month, let's skip that one!

We Do Not Know Their Price

Now this is JUST so I know where to start shopping policies for you, so should I start shopping in the range between $100 to $150 a month?

They Said They Are Price Sensitive

I know you had some price concerns already, and this next question is just so I know where I should start shopping for you, so should I start shopping in the range between $80 to $100 a month?

First, we need to know what form of payment the client will use. Some carriers will not accept checkless checking accounts like Direct Express, Chime Card, etc., while others will. The worst thing you can do is sell a policy that cannot take her form of payment, then have to backpedal and risk losing the sale.

Second, I advocate the "sell the premium" strategy for final expense agents. In general, your prospects want as much coverage as they can afford. And most of your clients buy products and services based on affordability. Selling the premium accomplishes this goal; it focuses your client's attention on budget as opposed to the amount of coverage they want.

A few important strategies we use:

- <u>Price Anchor:</u> Notice how we mention a $400 monthly premium. We do this to position our premiums as more affordable. When you reference a very high price that's out of reach for most, it makes the forthcoming premiums sound more reasonable than if we did not mention the price anchor. The result is your prospect will accept our price points more readily and with less friction.

- <u>Start High:</u> We also like to start high with our premiums. For example, we ask if the client can afford $100 to $150 a month, then move to lower premiums if the client cannot with full confidence commit to that price. We've found it's much easier to start high and go lower versus starting low then going higher. You'll have many more angry prospects that won't buy from you if you low ball your price then tell them they'll have to pay a premium much higher than they thought.

After the prospect selects a premium they can easily afford, it's time to pivot to your pricing and underwriting tool to figure out how much coverage their premium can give them:

<u>"Okay, so how much coverage are you looking to get?"</u>

<u>"Okay go get something to write these price-quotes down with... pen paper"</u>

Have your prospect write down the prices so they can more easily choose what works best.

We recommend showing three price points as follows:

- <u>First Option:</u> Low end of the prospect's budget
- <u>Second Option:</u> High end of the prospect's budget
- <u>Third Option:</u> An interval outside of the prospect's budget.

For example, if the prospect agreed to a $80 to $100 budget, I'll show coverage amounts that equate to an $80, $100, and $120 monthly premium.

Product Differentiation

After we share quotes, it's time to sell your prospect on why doing business with you today is the superior choice:

<u>**<FIRST NAME>** Okay, here's the price, I just want to make sure we choose the right product for you. Do you know the difference between Term and Whole Life? (term terminates, whole life is for your whole life)</u>

<u>"So, your coverage NEVER cancels and monthly payment NEVER goes up with this product"</u>

To clarify, we explain how our final expense product is whole life coverage that lasts your whole life and never goes up in price, unlike term insurance that gets more expensive and most likely will cancel before you pass away, leaving you with no peace of mind.

Once your prospect understands the benefits of your product, it's time to close the sale:

Getting to price now, <FIRST NAME> you don't have to pay anything today. <wait, confirm they heard you>

Also, any of the pricing options is okay to choose, higher or lower is totally fine. All we have to do from here is submit your application to the insurance company to make sure you actually get an approval <wait>

You can choose whichever amount of coverage you want, you're the one in control. Here we go, you ready for me to tell you the prices? <Tell them prices biggest to smallest, after they write them down...>

My job is just to submit the application and see if you can get approval, so which one do you want to get approval for?

At this point, you transition into the electronic or verbal application to medically qualify the client.

Rebuttal Closing Objections

As in the opening script, you'll experience objections as you attempt to close. Below I will describe the two most common closing objections and how to rebut.

Social Security Number

Many people are very uncomfortable with giving out their Social Security Number. Here's how you respond to that:

I can understand that, and here's the thing. Bottom line, you know you need coverage, right? You've told me as much, considering you've talked about wanting your loved ones to have peace of mind and not worry about paying for this expense. And in order for us to get you approved, the company has to pull medical records. And the way EVERY insurance company does it is by using your Social."

"Rest assured, you're privacy 100% safe because your information is stored with the carrier, and not me, if I don't live up to my promise, I will lose my livelihood and will not be able to put food on my table and take care of my kids, as ALL companies take your information seriously and aggressively fire agents who don't."

"So what's your Social?"

I Need To Get Off the Phone

This is VERY common to hear, as most people don't want to enter a sales call unexpectedly. Here's how to handle that, because again, this is a one-call sale business. You don't want them to get off the phone, because you aren't likely going to get a sale after they hang up:

*Oh you gotta go? No problem. Actually that's great, because I'm just a few minutes from the quote, so hang in there and I'll get you the price in just a few minutes. So... **[continue with script with the assumption they agree]***

-OR-

*Yup, I hear you. I gotta go here in a few minutes too. Actually, I'm just about to get you the price, so just hang in there and we'll be done real soon. So... **[continue with script with the assumption they agree]***

-OR-

*Yeah that's no problem. You can just take me with you in your ear so we can get this done. I need maybe a few minutes to get you the price, we're almost done. So... **[continue with script with the assumption they agree]***

Heads up: If you enjoyed this script, we go into even more detail on Insurance Sales Success. Registration is free and there's tons of free final expense remote sales training available at your fingertips. You can head over to www.davidduford.com/iss/ to get started.

Chapter 12: Putting It All Together: The Blueprint For Success

Alright, you did it! You made it through the book and you are ready to start your new life selling final expense insurance remotely in the comfort of your home.

As we finish, here are my final thoughts on what you need to do to maximize your chances at success:

1. <u>One Hundred Percent Commitment Is Critical.</u> Don't sell final expense unless you can commit completely. Whether you're part- or full-time, you must have a total commitment to the business. Understand this isn't a get rich quick scheme. This business isn't for everybody, and it's not for the faint of heart.

2. <u>Have Multiple Carrier Options.</u> Regardless of the agency you join, I recommend selecting three to five final expense carriers for maximal pricing and underwriting flexibility. Additionally, make sure you have a guaranteed-issue option as well to cover otherwise uninsurable prospects.

3. <u>Kill Your Ego.</u> I cannot overstate how humility and coachability are a must! What all top-producing agents have in common is their willingness to accept constructive criticism and rapidity in learning from their mistakes. Few

top producers are "naturals" in my experience, and instead accept being uncomfortable in order to experience growth.

4. <u>Keep It Simple.</u> Don't overcomplicate final expense remote sales. Instead, keep it simple. Follow a proven script and work a proven lead system. Resist the urge to reinvent the wheel. In short, if you're a part of a great agency, it's in your best interest to follow the system and do what you're told.

5. <u>Find A Great Agency Partner.</u> Selling final expense successfully requires that you find an agency and mentor that you can trust. Remember to do your due diligence! Picking the wrong agency or the wrong mentor can doom your career before it starts.

Thank you so much for reading my book. I wish you unparalleled success in this business, and pray that you'll work hard and find your way to the top. I'll see you there!

Appendix: FAQ

In this section, I included some frequently asked questions new agents ask about the final expense business.

Q: Can younger people take a final expense policy?
A: Absolutely! But you don't necessarily want that as a target. It's better to go for an older population for a larger premium size.

Q: What's the maximum age for a final expense policy?
A: Usually around 89 and or 90.

Q: Can a parent take out a final expense policy on their children?
A: Yes, although if they are adults, they will have to consent first

Q: Is it legal to text my leads?
A: You want to get to leads as quickly as possible, so something that helps is to text first rather than call. You can text them to get them on the phone, and then go into the pitch. Just make sure you're staying fully compliant with TCPA guidelines on texting first and foremost.

Q: How does the payout work once the policy holder has passed?
A: When a client dies, the beneficiary usually contacts the agent or the insurance carrier to file a death claim. Sometimes the funeral home helps with this. The carrier will check medical records to make sure there has been no misrepresentation, then pays the claim if everything checks out.

Q: How many leads do you need per week as a final expense remote agent?
A: When you are starting out, I recommend most agents to join a free lead program where you can get endless access to leads. If you insist on buying your own leads, I prefer Facebook-generated leads and recommend full-time agents work 100 or more leads weekly.

Appendix: Glossary

In this appendix, I included a list of industry-specific terms and acronyms you'll hear while doing your due diligence. Some of these terms are specific to final expense, while others are not. Thank you to [Tips, Tricks & Closers](#) for providing this list. You can learn more about them at ttcleads.com.

Policy-Related Definitions & Acronyms

- **Annual premium (AP):** Total premium paid for the year to cover the policy.
- **Monthly bank draft (MBD):** The monthly bank draft against the account.
- **Automated Clearing House (ACH):** Another phrase for "bank draft."
- **Issue Paid (IP):** A business that's been approved and issued.
- **Simplified Issue (SI):** An issue with no medical underwriting, but determined through the review of medical information or prescription check without an exam.
- **Cash Value (CV):** The value of a whole life policy over time.
- **Direct Express (DE):** A form of payment through a checkless checking account.
- **Social Security Billing (SSB):** Social Security deposit billing, where payments are drafted on the date SS payments are made.
- **Medical Information Bureau (MIB):** Where all Social Security information is stored, as well as any claims made against health insurance. The information can be checked

to support underwriting.
- **Level coverage:** First day, full, natural and accidental death coverage through insurance.
- **Preferred/standard:** A higher insurance rate class.
- **Graded/modified:** Partial coverage for an insurance product, such as a return of a premium.

Types Of Policies Definition/Acronyms

- **FE or FEX** - Final Expense
- **MP** - Mortgage Protection. Typically term life insurance that is sold as to pay off a mortgage in the case of premature death.
- **WL** - Whole Life. Coverage that lasts your whole life, typically with a fixed premium. Final expense policies are whole life policies.
- **TL** - Term Life. Coverage that lasts for a predetermined length of time. It's rare that final expense agents sell term life to their prospects.
- **UL** - Universal Life. A more customizable life insurance product that allows you to adjust premiums and coverage length as needed. This is rarely sold to final expense prospects.
- **GI** - Guaranteed Issue. This product guarantees insurability regardless of health as long as the client's age matches the product's requirement. Final expense agents should have at least one guaranteed issue product available to sell.
- **P&C** - Property and Casualty insurance. Think car and home insurance.
- **ROP** - Return of Premium. Final expense whole life insurance that pays back the premiums plus interest when a client dies, usually within the first two years.
- **AD&D** - Accidental Death and Dismemberment.

Insurance that pays out according to an accidental death or when the client loses limbs. Some agents sell this as an upsell to increase total coverage.

Agent-Related Acronyms/Definitions

- **LOA** - Licensed Only Agent: Commissions are paid to the agency, not to the agency directly.
- **Vested** - Agents that own their book of business.
- **Release** - Requesting to move your carrier contacts from one agency to another.
- **Captive** - Owned by an agency with one carrier product.
- **Independent** - Able to sell multiple carriers and work with multiple agencies.
- **CRM** - Customer Relationship Manager.

Agency Acronyms/Definitions

- **MLM** - Multilevel marketing: Agencies that are trying to monetize not off the sale of selling insurance, but off of buying leads or personal referrals.
- **IMO** - Independent Marketing Organization: A large organization that typically has other agencies underneath it that recruit agents.
- **FMO** - Field Marketing Organization: Typically a smaller version of an IMO.
- **NMO** - National Marketing Organization: A group of many FMOs and IMOs.
- **F2F** - Face to face
- **B2B** - Business to Business

Leads Acronyms/Definitions

- **FB Leads** - Facebook Leads. Most common way final

expense remote agents get leads.
- **DM** - Direct Mail. Mostly used by non-remote final expense agents.
- **LT** - Live Transfers. Leads that call you such as those generated from television commercials.
- **ROI** - Return on Investment. How much profit made from your investment.
- **CPL** - Cost Per Lead
- **CPA** - Cost Per Acquisition. How much money you must spend to acquire a new final expense client

Compliance Related Definitions/Acronyms

- **HIPAA** - Health Insurance Portability and Accountability Act. Final expense prospects must consent to have their health checked according to HIPAA guidelines.
- **CE** - Continuing Education. States require continuing education completion, typically every two years to keep your insurance license.
- **DOI** - Department of Insurance. Insurance law is state-run, and each state has a department of insurance.
- **DNC** - Do Not Call. Refers to leads you cannot call because they have opted out of receiving communications.
- **TCPA** - Telephone Consumer Protection Act. This is the legal doctrine protecting consumers from telemarketing abuse.

Join Our Team of New and Experienced Insurance Agents and Become a Top Producer!

Are you looking to excel in a rewarding career selling final expense insurance over the phone? Whether you're new to the industry or an experienced agent, The DIG Agency is your best choice for success!

Why Join The DIG Agency?

- **World-Class Training:** No experience? No problem! We'll provide comprehensive training to get you up to speed, even if you've never sold insurance before.
- **Free High-Quality Leads:** Forget about paying for leads! We provide you with an endless supply of free, high-quality leads through our proprietary lead generation system.
- **Remote Sales Focus:** Sell from the comfort of your

home—no in-person visits required. Our systems are optimized for remote, phone-based sales.
- **Access to Multiple Carriers:** With The DIG Agency, you'll have access to numerous carriers, enabling you to offer the best options for your clients and maximize your earnings.
- **Six-Figure Income Potential:** Many of our agents are on track to earn six-figure incomes by following our proven system. We're here to help you achieve the same success.
- **Low Start-Up Costs:** All you need to get started is a life insurance license and a few non-resident state licenses.

Ready To Learn More?

Visit www.DavidDuford.com to explore this opportunity and apply today!

30+ Hours Insurance Sales Training, Scripts, Books, And $1500+ In Free Bonuses... Yours FREE!

The Insurance Sales Success group is a no-cost, FREE insurance sales and marketing forum and training site, designed to provide the best resources for new and experienced agents on becoming a top producer.

Here's what you get as a no-cost member of the Insurance Sales Success group:

- 30+ hours of "deep dive" sales and marketing training on video for final expense, Medicare, health insurance, and annuities. This IS The Insurance Industry's MOST Comprehensive Training, Available To You For FREE!
- The Industry's BEST Live Zoom Meetings. Topics Include: Top Producer Interviews, Insurance Product Overviews, Open Mic Q&As, Lead Generation Tips, & Deep Dive Trainings On Insurance Sales & Marketing

- Interactive community of like-minded, growth-oriented agents, looking to grow their business and experience success selling insurance.

Extra Bonuses For You When You Join FOR FREE:

- David Duford's 3 Best-Selling Insurance Sales & Marketing E-Books ($50 Value, Yours FREE)
- FREE Final Expense Carrier Cheat Sheet To Help You Underwrite And Close More Presentations And Make MORE Money.
- Scripts GALORE: The EXACT Final Expense Presentation Script (Telesales & Face-To-Face), Appointment Setting, And Door Knocking Scripts Duford Insurance Group Agents Use! ($499 Value)
- David's Seminar Marketing Mastery Program. Learn How To Generate High-Intent, Cost Free Insurance Leads! ($499 Value)
- DIG's Annuity Trainer's Fact-Finding Training And Worksheet To Help You Find And Close More 4- And 5-Figure Annuities ($99 Value)
- Discounts On Insurance Pre-Licensing, AHIP Medicare Credentialing, And Helpful Insurance Software ($99 Value)

Ready to get started? Go to www.DavidDuford.com/iss/ to register now for free!

www.ingramcontent.com/pod-product-compliance
Lightning Source LLC
Chambersburg PA
CBHW071101240526
45471CB00016B/2289